contents

cheers 2

recipes 4

glossary 60

conversion chart 62

index 63

Please note that Australian cup and
spoon measurements are metric.
A conversion chart appears on page 62.

Cheers!

Store-bought drinks and juices are convenient, but take a little time to prepare a drink at home and it will leave the store-made version for dead. The recipes in this book will walk you through juice combinations, smoothies, lassis and frappés to kickstart your day, iced drinks to quench a summer thirst, punches that will really get the party started, and some hot and spicy drinks to help you nod off in front of a glowing fire in winter.

equipment

Most of the drinks in this book are made using either a blender or a juice extractor. Juices and smoothies prepared in a blender contain a good dose of fibre as the fruit/vegetable pulp is mixed through the drink; drinks prepared in a juice extractor, however, contain only the juice.

Blenders are best suited to soft fruits, such as mangoes, stone fruit, bananas and berries, especially when milk, yogurt or crushed ice is being added. Basically, they are ideal for the preparation of smoothies, lassis and frappés.

Juice extractors are ideal for use with hard fruit and vegetables such as apples, citrus, carrot, celery and other leafy greens.

An important consideration when purchasing a blender or juice extractor is how easy it is to keep clean. Any appliance you use for juicing and/or blending should be cleaned immediately, otherwise the fruit pulp can prove very difficult to remove.

drinks by definition

smoothie

A smoothie is a combination of fruit and dairy products, such as milk, ice-cream or yogurt, that is blended until thick and smooth.

frappé

A frappé is a frozen flavoured liquid (usually a blend of whole fruit – mangoes, pineapple, etc – or fruit juice with crushed ice) that has a slushy consistency.

lassi

A lassi is an Indian version of a milkshake, except that yogurt is used in place of milk. A variety of spices and fruits can be added to lend their distinctive flavours; other common additives are crushed ice or water. It is often served as a cooling accompaniment to a curry.

cucumber, celery, apple and spinach juice

1 telegraph cucumber (400g), chopped coarsely
2 trimmed celery stalks (200g), chopped coarsely
2 large green apples (400g), cored, chopped coarsely
50g baby spinach leaves, stems removed
1 cup (250ml) water
⅓ cup firmly packed fresh mint leaves

1 Blend ingredients, in batches, until pureed; strain through coarse sieve into large jug.

makes 1 litre (4 cups)
per 250ml 0.3g fat (0g saturated); 230kJ (55 cal); 11.9g carb
tips Refrigerate all ingredients before making the juice.
Serve the juice within 30 minutes of making.

papaya, strawberry and orange juice

1 large papaya (1.2kg),
    chopped coarsely
250g strawberries
¾ cup (180ml) fresh
    orange juice

1 Blend papaya, strawberries
and orange juice until smooth.

makes 1 litre (4 cups)
per 250ml 0.3g fat
(0g saturated); 368kJ
(88 cal); 19.4g carb
tips Refrigerate all ingredients
before making the juice.
Serve the juice within
30 minutes of making.

orange, carrot and ginger juice

1 large orange (300g), peeled,
    chopped coarsely
1 small carrot (70g),
    halved lengthways
2cm piece fresh ginger (10g)

1 Push orange, carrot and
ginger through juice extractor.
Stir to combine.

makes 1 cup (250ml)
per 250ml 0.3g fat
(0g saturated); 439kJ
(105 cal); 22.2g carb
tips Refrigerate all ingredients
before making the juice.
Serve the juice within
30 minutes of making.

tropical delight

You need about 400g of peeled and chopped pineapple for this recipe.

1 small pineapple (800g), peeled, chopped coarsely
4 medium apples (600g), chopped coarsely
2 medium oranges (480g), peeled, chopped coarsely

1 Push fruit through juice extractor. Stir to combine.

makes 1 litre (4 cups)
per 250ml 0.3g fat (0g saturated);
548kJ (131 cal); 30g carb
tips Refrigerate all ingredients before
making the juice.
Serve the juice within 30 minutes of making.

tomato, carrot and red capsicum juice

1 medium red capsicum (250g), chopped coarsely
4 medium tomatoes (300g), chopped coarsely
2 medium carrots (240g), chopped coarsely
⅓ cup firmly packed fresh flat-leaf parsley
1 cup (250ml) water
dash Tabasco sauce

1 Blend capsicum, tomato, carrot, parsley and water, in batches, until pureed; strain through coarse sieve into large jug.
2 Stir in Tabasco.

makes 1 litre (4 cups)
per 250ml 0.2g fat (0g saturated); 146kJ (35 cal); 6.1g carb
tips Refrigerate all ingredients before making the juice.
Serve the juice within 30 minutes of making.

mango and grapefruit juice

½ medium mango (215g),
    skinned, chopped coarsely
1 small grapefruit (350g),
    juiced
¼ cup (60ml) water

1 Blend ingredients
until smooth.

makes 1 cup (250ml)
per 250ml 0.8g fat
(0g saturated); 635kJ
(152 cal); 31.2g carb
tips Refrigerate all ingredients
before making the juice.
Serve the juice within
30 minutes of making.
Alternatively, for a refreshing
granita-like snack, freeze
the juice until almost frozen
then quickly mix with a fork
before drinking.

watermelon and mint juice

450g watermelon flesh,
    chopped coarsely
4 mint leaves

1 Blend ingredients
until smooth.

makes 1 cup (250ml)
per 250ml 1g fat
(0g saturated); 447kJ
(107 cal); 22.9g carb
tips Refrigerate all ingredients
before making the juice.
Serve the juice within
30 minutes of making.

beetroot, carrot and spinach juice

1 small beetroot (100g), chopped coarsely
1 small carrot (70g), chopped coarsely
1 cup firmly packed baby spinach leaves (20g)
½ cup (125ml) water

1 Push beetroot, carrot and spinach through
juice extractor. Dilute with the water; stir to combine.

makes 1 cup (250ml)
per 250ml 0.2g fat (0g saturated); 230kJ
(55 cal); 10.8g carb
tips Refrigerate all ingredients before
making the juice.
Serve the juice within 30 minutes of making.

fruity vegetable juice

2 medium beetroot (600g), trimmed, quartered
3 trimmed celery sticks (225g)
3 medium carrots (360g), halved lengthways
2 small apples (260g), quartered
2 medium oranges (480g), peeled, quartered

1 Push ingredients through juice extractor.
Stir to combine.

makes 1 litre (4 cups)
per 250ml 0.4g fat (0g saturated); 602kJ
(144 cal); 30.6g carb
tips Refrigerate all ingredients before making the juice.
Serve the juice within 30 minutes of making.
For a more tart drink, substitute 1 large grapefruit
(500g) for the oranges.

mixed berry smoothie

250ml frozen low-fat
    strawberry yogurt,
    softened slightly
1⅓ cups (200g) frozen
    mixed berries
3 cups (750ml) no-fat milk

1 Blend ingredients, in
batches, until smooth.
2 Serve immediately.

makes 1 litre (4 cups)
per 250ml 3.6g fat
(2.3g saturated); 803kJ
(192 cal); 27.9g carb

banana passionfruit soy smoothie

You need about six passionfruit for this recipe.

½ cup (125ml)
   passionfruit pulp
2 cups (500ml) soy milk
2 medium ripe bananas
   (400g), chopped coarsely

1 Strain passionfruit pulp through sieve into small bowl; reserve liquid and seeds.
2 Blend passionfruit liquid, milk and banana, in batches, until smooth.
3 Pour smoothie into large jug; stir in reserved seeds.

makes 1 litre (4 cups)
per 250ml 4.7g fat (0.5g saturated); 656kJ (157 cal); 22.5g carb

banana smoothie

2 cups (500ml) no-fat milk
2 medium bananas (400g), chopped coarsely
½ cup (140g) low-fat yogurt
1 tablespoon honey
1 tablespoon wheat germ
¼ teaspoon ground cinnamon

1 Blend ingredients until smooth.

makes 1 litre (4 cups)
per 250ml 0.9g fat (0.5g saturated); 698kJ
(167 cal); 30.5g carb

sweet saffron lassi

*Lassis are yogurt-based drinks which are an
excellent cooling foil for a fiery Indian curry.*

pinch saffron threads
1 tablespoon boiling water
2 cups (560g) yogurt
1 cup (250ml) iced water
2 tablespoons caster sugar
½ teaspoon ground cardamom
ice cubes

1 Combine saffron and the boiling water in
small heatproof cup; stand 5 minutes.
2 Whisk yogurt, the iced water, sugar and
cardamom in large jug; stir in saffron mixture.
3 Serve lassi over ice cubes.

makes 3 cups (750ml)
per 250ml 6.4g fat (4.1g saturated); 782kJ
(187 cal); 22.1g carb

coconut mango thickshake

3 medium mangoes (1.3kg)
200ml can coconut milk
1½ cups (375ml) milk
500ml vanilla ice-cream, chopped

1 Cut mango flesh from both sides of the seed. Remove the skin and freeze mango for several hours or until firm.
2 Blend milks, mango and ice-cream, in two batches, until smooth. Serve immediately.

serves 6
per serving 14.1g fat (10.6g saturated); 1145kJ (274 cal); 31.9g carb
tip For a reduced-fat version of the thickshake, substitute light coconut milk, no-fat milk and low-fat ice-cream. You can also use peaches, nectarines, plums, apricots, bananas or berries, or a combination if you prefer, instead of the mango.

pineapple orange frappé

1 medium pineapple (1.25kg),
   chopped coarsely
½ cup (125ml) orange juice
3 cups crushed ice
1 tablespoon finely grated
   orange rind

1 Blend pineapple and juice,
in batches, until smooth.
2 Pour into large jug with
crushed ice and rind; stir to
combine. Serve immediately.

makes 1 litre (4 cups)
per 250ml 0.2g fat
(0g saturated); 309kJ
(74 cal); 16g carb

mango frappé

2 medium mangoes (860g)
3 cups ice cubes
1 tablespoon sugar

1 Halve mangoes, peel, then discard seeds. Blend or process mango flesh with ice cubes and sugar until thick and smooth.
2 Pour into serving glasses; stand at room temperature for 5 minutes before serving.

makes 3 cups (750ml)
per 250ml 0.4g fat (0g saturated); 569kJ (136 cal); 31.3g carb

minted tomato, rhubarb and lime frappé

4 cups chopped rhubarb (440g)
¼ cup (55g) sugar
¼ cup (60ml) water
4 medium tomatoes (760g), peeled,
   seeded, chopped
2½ tablespoons lime juice
3 cups ice cubes
2 tablespoons chopped fresh mint

1 Combine rhubarb, sugar and the water in medium saucepan; simmer, covered, about 10 minutes or until rhubarb is tender. Cool.
2 Blend or process rhubarb mixture with remaining ingredients until smooth; serve immediately.

makes 1.25 litres (5 cups)
per 250ml 0.4g fat (0g saturated); 334kJ (80 cal); 15.4g carb

fresh berry frappé

300g blueberries
250g raspberries
4 cups crushed ice
1 cup (250ml) fresh
   orange juice

1 Blend berries until just
smooth. Push berry puree
through fine sieve into large
bowl; discard solids in sieve.
2 Stir in ice and juice and
spoon into serving glasses;
serve immediately.

makes 1 litre (4 cups)
per 250ml 0.4g fat
(0g saturated); 338kJ
(81 cal); 17g carb
tips Depending of the
sweetness of the berries,
you may need to add sugar.
You can crush the ice in a
blender or food processor.
You can also use frozen
berries for this recipe.
Experiment with other berries
– strawberries, blackberries,
boysenberries – and adjust
combinations to your taste.

raspberry cranberry crush

1 cup (250ml) raspberry sorbet
2 cups (500ml) cranberry juice
1 cup (150g) frozen
   raspberries
2 tablespoons lemon juice

1 Blend or process
ingredients until smooth;
serve immediately.

makes 1 litre (4 cups)
per 250ml 0.2g fat
(0g saturated); 543kJ
(130 cal); 31.1g carb
tip Add a little icing sugar if
you prefer this drink sweeter.

iced mocha

1 tablespoon instant coffee powder
1 tablespoon boiling water
2 tablespoons chocolate-flavoured topping
1½ cups (375ml) cold milk
4 scoops (500ml) vanilla ice-cream
½ cup (125ml) cream, whipped
1 teaspoon drinking chocolate

1 Combine coffee and the water in large
heatproof jug, stir until dissolved.
2 Stir in chocolate-flavoured topping and milk.
Pour into two large glasses and top each with
2 scoops vanilla ice-cream and cream, then sprinkle
with sifted drinking chocolate; serve immediately.

serves 2
per serving 43.9g fat (28.7g saturated);
2696kJ (645 cal); 52.7g carb

spiced iced coffee milkshake

¼ cup (20g) ground espresso coffee
¾ cup (180ml) boiling water
2 cardamom pods, bruised
¼ teaspoon ground cinnamon
1 tablespoon brown sugar
3 scoops (375ml) low-fat vanilla ice-cream
2½ cups (625ml) no-fat milk

1 Place coffee then the water in coffee plunger; stand 2 minutes before plunging. Pour coffee into small heatproof bowl with cardamom, cinnamon and sugar; stir to dissolve sugar then cool 10 minutes.
2 Strain coffee mixture through fine sieve into blender or processor; process with ice-cream and milk until smooth. Serve immediately.

makes 1 litre (4 cups)
per 250ml 3g fat (2g saturated);
640kJ (153 cal); 21.6g carb

vanilla cafe latte

⅓ cup (30g) coarsely ground
   coffee beans
500ml (2 cups) milk
1 teaspoon vanilla extract

1 Combine ingredients
in medium saucepan, stir,
over low heat until heated
through, but not boiling.
2 Pour through fine strainer
into heatproof serving glasses.

serves 2
per serving 9.9g fat
(6.5g saturated); 765kJ
(183 cal); 13.6g carb

spiced chocolate milk

30g dark eating chocolate, melted
2 cups (500ml) milk
1 cinnamon stick

1 Using a teaspoon, drizzle melted chocolate onto the insides of heatproof glasses.
2 Combine milk and cinnamon stick in medium saucepan, stir over low heat until heated through, but not boiling. Remove cinnamon. Pour milk into glasses.

serves 2
per serving 14.1g fat (9g saturated); 1020kJ (244 cal); 21.5g carb

real hot chocolate

1 litre (4 cups) milk
200g milk eating chocolate, chopped
100g dark eating chocolate, chopped
¾ cup (180ml) thickened cream
1 tablespoon Tia Maria or Baileys Irish Cream
90g Maltesers, chopped

1 Combine milk and both chocolates in medium saucepan; stir over low heat until chocolate is melted. Do not boil milk.
2 Beat cream and liqueur in small bowl of electric mixer until soft peaks form.
3 Divide milk among heatproof serving glasses, top with cream mixture and sprinkle with Maltesers.

serves 6
per serving 35.3g fat (24g saturated); 2328kJ (557 cal); 50.6g carb

masala chai

For this spicy traditional Indian milk tea, we used
English Breakfast tea – but try experimenting with
other varieties until you find one that suits your taste.

2 cinnamon sticks
1 teaspoon cardamom pods, bruised
1 teaspoon fennel seeds
½ teaspoon whole cloves
1 teaspoon ground ginger
½ teaspoon ground nutmeg
½ cup firmly packed fresh mint leaves
4 teabags
2 cups (500ml) milk
2 cups (500ml) water
sugar

1 Combine spices, mint and teabags in
teapot or heatproof jug. Bring combined milk
and water to a boil, pour over spice mixture;
stand 10 minutes.
2 Sweeten with a little sugar, if desired.
Just before serving, strain.

makes 1 litre (4 cups)
per 250ml 5g fat (3.2g saturated); 418kJ
(100 cal); 9.8g carb

spiced tea punch

1 litre (4 cups) water
4 teabags
1 cinnamon stick
2 cardamom pods
4 whole cloves
1 cup (220g) caster sugar
1½ cups (375ml) cold water, extra
½ cup (125ml) fresh lemon juice
2 cups (500ml) fresh orange juice
1 medium lemon (140g), sliced
¼ cup coarsely chopped fresh mint
1 litre (4 cups) mineral water
ice cubes

1 In a large saucepan, bring the water to a boil; add teabags, spices and sugar. Stir over low heat for about 3 minutes or until sugar is dissolved; discard teabags. Refrigerate until cold.
2 Discard spices then stir in the extra water, juices, lemon and mint. Just before serving, add mineral water and ice cubes.

makes 3 litres (12 cups)
per 250ml 0.1g fat (0g saturated); 376kJ (90 cal); 22g carb
tip The tea mixture can be made a day ahead; store, covered, in the refrigerator.

tropical punch

You need half a medium pineapple, weighing approximately 650g, for this recipe.

425g can sliced mango in natural juice
3 cups (750ml) tropical fruit juice
300g finely chopped pineapple
250g finely chopped strawberries
2 tablespoons finely shredded fresh mint
1 tablespoon caster sugar
3 cups (750ml) dry ginger ale

1 Strain mango over small bowl; reserve juice. Chop mango slices finely; combine mango and reserved juice in large bowl with tropical fruit juice. Stir in pineapple, strawberries, mint, sugar and ginger ale.
2 Refrigerate punch 2 hours before serving.

makes 2.5 litres (10 cups)
per 250ml 0.1g fat (0g saturated); 314kJ (75 cal); 17.7g carb

tomato, apple and ginger punch

1 medium red apple (150g)
8cm piece fresh ginger (40g), grated finely
125g strawberries, quartered
2 cups (500ml) apple juice
1½ cups (375ml) tomato juice
3 cups (750ml) dry ginger ale

1 Core and chop apple. Over small bowl, press ginger between two teaspoons to extract juice; discard pulp. Combine apple and strawberries in large jug, add ginger juice and remaining juices; mix well.
2 Cover, refrigerate until cold. Just before serving, add cold ginger ale.

makes 2 litres (8 cups)
per 250ml 0.1g fat (0g saturated); 355kJ (85 cal); 21g carb
tip This recipe can be made a day ahead, but hold off on adding the ginger ale until just before serving.

mixed berry punch

1 teabag
1 cup (250ml) boiling water
120g raspberries
150g blueberries
125g strawberries, halved
¼ cup loosely packed fresh mint leaves
750ml chilled sparkling apple cider
2½ cups (625ml) chilled lemonade

1 Place teabag in heatproof mug, cover with the water; stand 10 minutes. Squeeze teabag over mug, discard teabag; cool tea 10 minutes.
2 Using fork, crush raspberries in punch bowl; add blueberries, strawberries, mint and tea. Stir to combine, cover; refrigerate 1 hour. Stir cider and lemonade into punch just before serving; sprinkle with extra mint leaves, if desired.

serves 8
per serving 0.1g fat (0g saturated); 422kJ (101 cal); 18.5g carb

sparkling fruity punch

2 litres (8 cups) orange and passionfruit juice drink
850ml can unsweetened pineapple juice
250g strawberries, chopped
¼ cup (60ml) passionfruit pulp
2 medium red apples (300g), chopped
2 medium oranges (360g), peeled, chopped
1.25 litres (5 cups) lemon soda squash
1.25 litres (5 cups) creaming soda
3 cups (750ml) ginger beer
fresh mint sprigs

1 Combine orange and passionfruit juice drink,
pineapple juice and fruit in large bowl.
2 Just before serving, stir in remaining ingredients.
Serve cold.

makes 6.5 litres (26 cups)
per 250ml 0.2g fat (0g saturated); 326kJ
(78 cal); 18.2g carb
tip Refrigerate all ingredients before making the
punch. Punch base can be prepared several hours
ahead; add sparkling drinks just before serving.

moroccan mint tea

1 litre (4 cups) hot water
3 teabags
1 cup loosely packed fresh
    mint leaves
2 tablespoons caster sugar
½ cup loosely packed fresh
    mint leaves, extra
1 cup ice cubes

1 Combine the water,
teabags, mint and sugar in
medium heatproof jug, stand
10 minutes; discard teabags.
Cover; refrigerate until cool.
2 Strain tea mixture; discard
leaves. Add extra mint and
ice cubes; serve immediately.

makes 1 litre (4 cups)
per 250ml 0.2g fat
(0g saturated); 176kJ
(42 cal); 9.8g carb

lemon iced tea

3 teabags
3 lemon soother or
  lemon zinger teabags
1.5 litres (6 cups) boiling water
⅓ cup (80g) caster sugar
2 strips of lemon rind
1 cup ice cubes

1 Combine teabags, the
water, sugar and rind in large
heatproof jug, stir until sugar
is dissolved; cool to room
temperature, strain mixture.
2 Refrigerate until cold.
Serve with ice cubes.

makes 1.5 litres (6 cups)
per 250ml 0g fat
(0g saturated); 217kJ
(52 cal); 13.4g carb

lemon grass and ginger iced tea

6 lemon grass and ginger teabags
1 litre (4 cups) boiling water
2 tablespoons grated palm sugar
10cm stick fresh lemon grass (20g), chopped finely
½ small orange (90g), sliced thinly
½ lemon, sliced thinly
¼ cup firmly packed fresh mint leaves, torn
1 cup ice cubes

1 Place teabags and the water in large
heatproof jug; stand 5 minutes.
2 Discard teabags. Add sugar, lemon grass,
orange and lemon to jug; stir to combine.
Refrigerate, covered, until cold.
3 Stir mint into cold tea; serve immediately
over ice.

makes 1 litre (4 cups)
per 250ml 0.1g fat (0g saturated); 159kJ
(38 cal); 8.5g carb

lime and mint spritzer

1 cup (250ml) lime juice
1.25 litres (5 cups) chilled mineral water
¼ cup coarsely chopped fresh mint
sugar syrup
½ cup (125ml) water
½ cup (110g) caster sugar

1 Make sugar syrup.
2 Combine syrup in large jug with juice,
mineral water and mint. Serve immediately,
with ice if desired.
sugar syrup Combine ingredients in
small saucepan; stir over heat until sugar
dissolves. Bring to a boil, remove from heat;
refrigerate until cold.

serves 8
per serving 0.1g fat (0g saturated); 252kJ
(60 cal); 14.2g carb

homemade lemonade

4 medium lemons (560g)
4 cups (880g) caster sugar
2 cups (500ml) water
5 litres (20 cups) mineral water

1 Remove rind from lemons using a vegetable peeler, avoiding white pith; reserve lemons. Combine rind, sugar and the water in large saucepan; stir over low heat, without boiling, until sugar is dissolved. Bring to a boil, simmer, uncovered, without stirring, about 10 minutes or until syrup is thickened slightly; cool.
2 Squeeze juice from lemons – you will need 1 cup (250ml) lemon juice. Add juice to syrup, strain into jug; cover, keep refrigerated.
3 Just before serving, add four parts mineral water to one part lemonade, or to taste.

makes 6.25 litres (25 cups) diluted lemonade or 1.25 litres (5 cups) undiluted lemonade
per 250ml (diluted) 0g fat (0g saturated); 293kJ (70 cal); 17.8g carb

glossary

apple, green we used granny smith apples – crisp, juicy apples with a rich green skin.

baileys irish cream a smooth and creamy natural blend of fresh Irish cream, the finest Irish spirits, Irish whiskey, cocoa and vanilla.

beetroot also known as red beets; firm, round root vegetable.

capsicum also known as bell pepper or, simply, pepper. They can be red, green, yellow, orange or purplish black. Seeds and membranes should be discarded before use.

cardamom native to India and used extensively in its cuisine; can be purchased in pod, seed or ground form. Has a distinctive aromatic, sweetly rich flavour and is one of the world's most expensive spices.

chocolate
dark eating: made of cocoa liquor, cocoa butter and sugar.

drinking chocolate: sweetened cocoa powder.
milk: we used eating-quality milk chocolate.

flavoured topping: used to flavour drinks and as a topping for desserts such as ice-cream.

cinnamon dried inner bark of the shoots of the cinnamon tree.

clove dried flower buds of a tropical tree; can be used whole or in ground form. Have a strong scent and taste so should be used minimally.

cream
fresh: (minimum fat content 35%) also known as pure cream and pouring cream; has no additives.
thickened: (minimum fat content 35%) whipping cream containing a thickener.

creaming soda a sweet carbonated drink.

fennel dried seeds having a licorice flavour.

ginger also known as green or root ginger; the thick gnarled root of a tropical plant. Can be kept,

peeled, covered with dry sherry in a jar and refrigerated, or frozen in an airtight container.

ginger ale a ginger-flavoured carbonated drink.

ginger, ground also known as powdered ginger; used as a flavouring in cakes, pies and puddings but cannot be substituted for fresh ginger.

lemon grass a tall, clumping, lemon-smelling and tasting, sharp-edged grass; the white lower part of the stem is used, finely chopped, in cooking.

lemon soda squash a lemon flavoured carbonated drink.

maltesers chocolates with crisp, light honeycomb centres; made from chocolate, glucose syrup, malt extract, milk powder, flour and sugar.

mango tropical fruit with skin colour ranging from green through yellow to deep red. Fragrant deep yellow flesh surrounds a large flat seed.

milk, coconut not the juice found inside the fruit, which is known as coconut water, but the diluted liquid from the second pressing from the white meat of a mature coconut (the first pressing produces coconut cream). Available in cans and cartons at supermarkets.

nectar thick fruit juice.

nutmeg is available in ground form or you can grate your own with a fine grater.

papaya also known as pawpaw, it's a large, pear-shaped red-orange tropical fruit. Sometimes used unripe (green) in cooking.

parsley, flat-leaf also known as continental parsley and italian parsley.

rhubarb thick, celery-like stalked vegetable, eaten as a fruit. Only the stalk is edible; the leaves are toxic and must not be eaten.

rind also known as zest.

saffron stigma of a member of the crocus family, available in strands or ground form; imparts a yellow-orange colour to food once infused. Quality varies greatly; the best is the most expensive spice in the world. Should be stored in the freezer.

spinach correct name for this leafy green vegetable; often called english spinach or, incorrectly, silverbeet.

sugar we used coarse, granulated table sugar, also known as crystal sugar, unless otherwise specified.

   brown: an extremely soft, fine granulated sugar retaining molasses for its characteristic colour and flavour.

   caster: also known as superfine or finely granulated table sugar.

   palm: also known as nam tan pip, jaggery, jawa or gula melaka; made from the sap of the sugar palm tree. Light brown to

black in colour and usually sold in rock-hard cakes; substitute it with brown sugar if unavailable.

tabasco brand name of an extremely fiery sauce made from vinegar, hot red peppers and salt.

telegraph cucumber long and green with ridges running down its entire length; also known as continental cucumber.

tia maria coffee-flavoured liqueur.

vanilla extract obtained from vanilla beans infused in water. A non-alcoholic version of essence.

vanilla ice-cream, low-fat we used an ice-cream containing 3% fat.

watermelon large green-skinned melon with crisp, juicy red flesh.

wheat germ small creamy flakes milled from the embryo of the wheat.

yogurt, low-fat we used yogurt with a fat content of less than 0.2%.

conversion chart

MEASURES

One Australian metric measuring cup holds approximately 250ml, one Australian metric tablespoon holds 20ml, one Australian metric teaspoon holds 5ml.

The difference between one country's measuring cups and another's is within a two- or three-teaspoon variance, and will not affect your cooking results. North America, New Zealand and the United Kingdom use a 15ml tablespoon.

All cup and spoon measurements are level. The most accurate way of measuring dry ingredients is to weigh them. When measuring liquids, use a clear glass or plastic jug with the metric markings.

We use large eggs with an average weight of 60g.

DRY MEASURES

METRIC	IMPERIAL
15g	½oz
30g	1oz
60g	2oz
90g	3oz
125g	4oz (¼lb)
155g	5oz
185g	6oz
220g	7oz
250g	8oz (½lb)
280g	9oz
315g	10oz
345g	11oz
375g	12oz (¾lb)
410g	13oz
440g	14oz
470g	15oz
500g	16oz (1lb)
750g	24oz (1½lb)
1kg	32oz (2lb)

LIQUID MEASURES

METRIC	IMPERIAL
30ml	1 fluid oz
60ml	2 fluid oz
100ml	3 fluid oz
125ml	4 fluid oz
150ml	5 fluid oz (¼ pint/1 gill)
190ml	6 fluid oz
250ml	8 fluid oz
300ml	10 fluid oz (½ pint)
500ml	16 fluid oz
600ml	20 fluid oz (1 pint)
1000ml (1 litre)	1¾ pints

LENGTH MEASURES

METRIC	IMPERIAL
3mm	⅛in
6mm	¼in
1cm	½in
2cm	¾in
2.5cm	1in
5cm	2in
6cm	2½in
8cm	3in
10cm	4in
13cm	5in
15cm	6in
18cm	7in
20cm	8in
23cm	9in
25cm	10in
28cm	11in
30cm	12in (1ft)

OVEN TEMPERATURES

These oven temperatures are only a guide for conventional ovens.
For fan-forced ovens, check the manufacturer's manual.

	°C (CELSIUS)	°F (FAHRENHEIT)	GAS MARK
Very slow	120	250	½
Slow	150	275 – 300	1 – 2
Moderately slow	160	325	3
Moderate	180	350 – 375	4 – 5
Moderately hot	200	400	6
Hot	220	425 – 450	7 – 8
Very hot	240	475	9

index

apple, cucumber, celery and
  spinach juice 4

banana passionfruit
  soy smoothie 19
banana smoothie 20
beetroot, carrot and
  spinach juice 15
berry frappé, fresh 30
berry punch, mixed 48
berry smoothie, mixed 18
blenders 3

cafe latte, vanilla 36
chocolate milk, spiced 37
coconut mango thickshake 24
cucumber, celery, apple and
  spinach juice 4

definitions
  frappé 3
  lassi 3
  smoothie 3

extractors, juice 3

frappé 3
frappés
  fresh berry 30
  mango 27
  minted tomato, rhubarb
    and lime 28
  pineapple orange 26
  raspberry cranberry crush 31
fresh berry frappé 30
fruity punch, sparkling 51
fruity vegetable juice 16

grapefruit juice, mango and 12

homemade lemonade 59
hot chocolate, real 39
hot drinks
  masala chai 40
  real hot chocolate 39
  spiced chocolate milk 37
  vanilla cafe latte 36

iced coffees
  iced mocha 32
  spiced iced coffee
    milkshake 35
iced mocha 32
iced teas
  lemon 53
  lemon grass and ginger 55
  moroccan mint tea 52

juice extractors 3
juices
  beetroot, carrot
    and spinach 15
  cucumber, celery, apple
    and spinach 4
  fruity vegetable 16
  mango and grapefruit 12
  orange, carrot and ginger 7
  papaya, strawberry
    and orange 6
  tomato, carrot and
    red capsicum 11
  tropical delight 8
  watermelon and mint 13

lassi 3
  sweet saffron 23
lemon grass and ginger
  iced tea 55
lemon iced tea 53
lemonade, homemade 59
lime and mint spritzer 56

mango and grapefruit juice 12
mango frappé 27
masala chai 40
milkshake, spiced iced coffee 35
minted tomato, rhubarb
  and lime frappé 28
mixed berry punch 48
mixed berry smoothie 18
mocha, iced 32
moroccan mint tea 52

orange juice, papaya,
  strawberry and 6

orange, carrot and
  ginger juice 7

papaya, strawberry
  and orange juice 6
pineapple orange frappé 26
punches
  mixed berry 48
  sparkling fruity 51
  spiced tea 43
  tomato, apple
    and ginger 47
  tropical 44

raspberry cranberry crush 31
real hot chocolate 39

saffron lassi, sweet 23
smoothie 3
smoothies
  banana 20
  banana passionfruit soy 19
  mixed berry 18
  sparkling fruity punch 51
  spiced chocolate milk 37
  spiced iced coffee
    milkshake 35
  spiced tea punch 43
  spritzer, lime and mint 56
  sweet saffron lassi 23

tea, moroccan mint 52
thickshake, coconut mango 24
tomato, apple and
  ginger punch 47
tomato, carrot and
  red capsicum juice 11
tomato, rhubarb and
  lime frappé, minted 28
tropical delight 8
tropical punch 44

vanilla cafe latte 36
vegetable juice, fruity 16

watermelon and
  mint juice 13

Are you missing some of the world's favourite cookbooks?

The Australian Women's Weekly cookbooks are available from bookshops, cookshops, supermarkets and other stores all over the world. You can also buy direct from the publisher, using the order form below.

MINI SERIES £3.50 190x138MM 64 PAGES

TITLE	QTY	TITLE	QTY	TITLE	QTY
4 Fast Ingredients		Gluten-free Cooking		Potatoes	
4 Kids 2 Cook		Grills & Barbecues		Quick Desserts	
15-minute Feasts		Healthy Everyday Food 4 Kids		Roast	
50 Fast Chicken Fillets		Ice-creams & Sorbets		Salads	
50 Fast Desserts		Indian Cooking		Simple Slices	
Barbecue Chicken		Italian Favourites		Simply Seafood	
Biscuits, Brownies & Bisottti		Indonesian Favourites		Soup plus	
Bites		Jams & Jellies		Spanish Favourites	
Bowl Food		Japanese Favourites		Stir-fries	
Burgers, Rösti & Fritters		Kebabs & Skewers		Stir-fry Favourites	
Cafe Cakes		Kids Party Food		Summer Salads	
Cafe Food		Lebanese Cooking		Tagines & Couscous	
Casseroles & Curries		Low-Fat Delicious		Tapas, Antipasto & Mezze	
Char-grills & Barbecues		Low Fat Fast		Tarts	
Cheesecakes, Pavlova & Trifles		Malaysian Favourites		Tex-Mex	
Chinese Favourites		Mince Favourites		Thai Favourites	
Chocolate Cakes		Microwave		The Fast Egg	
Crumbles & Bakes		Muffins		The Young Chef	
Cupcakes & Cookies		Noodles & Stir-fries		Vegetarian	
Dips & Dippers		Old-Fashioned Desserts		Vegie Main Meals	
Dried Fruit & Nuts		Outdoor Eating		Vietnamese Favourites	
Drinks		Packed Lunch		Wok	
Easy Pies & Pastries		Party Food			
Fast Fillets		Pickles and Chutneys			
Fishcakes & Crispybakes		Pasta		TOTAL COST £	

Photocopy and complete coupon below

Name _____

Address _____

_____ Postcode _____

Country _____ Phone (business hours) _____

Email*(optional) _____

*By including your email address, you consent to receipt of any email regarding this magazine, and other emails which inform you of ACP's other publications, products, services and events, and to promote third party goods and services you may be interested in.

I enclose my cheque/money order for £ _____ or please charge £ _____

to my: ☐ Access ☐ Mastercard ☐ Visa ☐ Diners Club

Card number | | | | | | | | | | | | | | | | |

3 digit security code *(found on reverse of card)* _____

Cardholder's signature _____ Expiry date ____ /____

To order: Mail or fax – photocopy or complete the order form above, and send your credit card details or cheque payable to: Australian Consolidated Press (UK), 10 Scirocco Close, Moulton Park Office Village, Northampton NN3 6AP, phone (+44) (01) 604 642200, fax (+44) (01) 604 642300, e-mail books@acpuk.com or order online at www.acpuk.com
Non-UK residents: We accept the credit cards listed on the coupon, or cheques, drafts or International Money Orders payable in sterling and drawn on a UK bank. Credit card charges are at the exchange rate current at the time of payment.
All pricing current at time of going to press and subject to change/availability.
Postage and packing UK: Add £1.00 per order plus 75p per book.
Postage and packing overseas: Add £2.00 per order plus £1.50 per book. **Offer ends 31.12.2008**